Why I wrote this book...

"Mommy, Daddy, why don't you two live together any~~~~~~ ~~ ~ ~~~~~~~~ ~~~~ we, separated parents, aren't really fully ready to answer. How can we tell our child, whose dearest wish is their family to be whole again, that their wish won't come true?

It was a question posed to me by my own 7-year-old daughter. I didn't want to tell her all the details of our separation. At the same time, I wanted to explain to her why we could no longer live together. So I started to tell her a story about the Sun Prince and the Moon Fairy. It's a story about two beings, both with their own unique light, a story about love, that sometimes cannot overcome all obstacles, and a story about love that remains forever – love for their star, their child.

Polona Kisovec, author

»To my darling little star, Ines. May you always find the answer to your why.«

Renowned child psychologist Dr. Amanda Gummer commented on the book's value:

"Children can have many mixed feelings when their parents separate or divorce and I applaud anyone who offers support and tools to help them understand the process and manage their feelings.

Storybooks such as the story of Moon Fairy and Sun Prince are a lovely, gentle way for children to understand that life can still be happy and fulfilling after parents separate. This is also a great way for parents to open-up conversations about their family arrangements; giving them the opportunity to talk to their children about the situation and explain how any changes will affect them and be implemented.

Young children often struggle to voice their concerns and anxieties as they may not have the vocabulary to express themselves in the way they'd like; similarly, older children may not want to talk directly about it for fear of upsetting their parents. Using fantasy characters such as the ones in the book give the children a way of thinking and talking about the situation without making it too personal or sad.

My recommendation is that parents first read this book together with their child and then, for those children who are old enough to read themselves, leave it somewhere accessible so they can return to it whenever they choose and re-read the parts of the story that are relevant to their situation or resonate with them."

Dr. Amanda Gummer biography

Amanda has a PhD in neuropsychology, the Postgraduate Certificate in Higher Education and over 20 years experience working with children and families. Widely considered as the UK's go to expert on play, toys and child development, she combines her theoretical knowledge with a refreshingly pragmatic approach to family life, that resonates both with parents and professionals. Her book 'Play' was published in May 2105 and has already been translated into two different languages with extracts being published in the USA's Toy Industry Association's Genius of Play initiative. Amanda is regularly in the media, continues to take an active role in research, and is often involved in government policy around children's issues - currently as a member of two All Party Parliamentary Groups. Amanda ran the research consultancy FUNdamentals for 10 years before combining that with the Good Toy Guide, and the Good App Guide to create Fundamentally Children, the UK's leading source of expert, independent advice on child development and play, supporting children's industries with research, insight and endorsement.

Parental Advice by Dr. Amanda Gummer

This storybook is intended as a fictional tool to help encourage conversation and reassurance that parental love, from both sides, doesn't alter despite a change in family circumstances.

1. Don't treat your child as a mini-adult, talk to him/her using age appropriate language.

2. Gradually explaining things and waiting for opportunities for discussions to arise naturally is better than giving a child too much information in one go; using this book as a tool is a good way of achieving this.

3. Remember young children are ego-centric and are mostly concerned with things that affect them - where they will live, how often they will see the non-resident parent etc. so start with those topics and then just answer questions as they arise, but ensure they know they will always be loved.

4. It's important to realise that every child adapts to change differently; it's important not to overwhelm them but also encourage them to be open with their feelings and provide ongoing reassurance that the situation is not their 'fault'.

5. Don't use children as an emotional prop when you feel low - it's fine to let them see you have feelings too, but it's not their role to make you feel better. Make sure you have a good support network.

6. Don't over-load children with information, let them lead the discussion and answer their questions simply and honestly which will hopefully be achieved from having conversations through reading this book together.

7. Read the book with your child and then leave it somewhere accessible for him/her to read again when he/she wants to do so.

8. Remember to ask your child how he/she feels and give children as much choice over decisions as possible (but if you give them the option to choose, you must stick with their choice, so it's best to avoid points which could cause issues if you can't be bound by their decision).

9. In periods of change, try and keep everything else in the children's lives as constant as possible.

10. Try and keep adult discussions and arguments away from children, they will worry about things they can't fully understand and can easily misinterpret conversations.

Why you should read this book...

MARKO JUHANT, *an expert in the field of education*

The most difficult part in the tragedy of a family breakdown is how to explain to children why their parents will no longer live together. A child feels his/her family is falling apart but is not able to understand it rationally. The confusion in their feelings and behaviour is therefore inevitable.

A story from the book can be really helpful in this confusion because it does not favour any of the parents, but emphasizes the role and the circumstances leading to the parents' separation. Every child ponders to what extent it is his/her fault the parents fought and separated. Children take on so much guilt without a reason! In the story about Moon Fairy and Sun Prince, a child learns that the little star is not responsible for everything that goes wrong. This brings them hope that what is happening in their family is not their fault. Fairytale is a perfect opportunity for the child to hear that both parents love him/her and that they will always be his/her mummy and daddy. They can tell the child that they tried but that they can no longer live together.

KATJA FORTUN, *social pedagogue and systemic psychotherapy specialist*

The book Shine is ready to come to life in families that are separating. Separation brings a lot of burden and stress into any family. Parents want to protect their children from the pain and many avoid conversation or make it quick and simply inform the child. However, children are very sensitive beings and have a great sense of family dynamics.

The subtle and sensual content of the book touches the reader or the listener, regardless of their age. The story also has soft and beautiful illustrations that help small children understand the world of adults and stimulate their imagination. I think the book Moon Fairy should be read in all separated families and especially in those in the process of separation.

IVONA KYSSELEF, *divorced mother*

I read the book cover to cover and had real goose bumps while reading it. A wonderful fairy tale, really beautiful and real! We experienced the same situation and our star is shining brighter every day. In my opinion, this story is not just for children, but for parents as well, especially for those who are afraid to get separated because of the children. They are not aware they can give much more to their child and make him/her happier if they separate and are both happy by themselves.

META VEDENIK, *grandmother*

I've read this wonderful book from cover to cover. After that I've gifted it to my grandson, who likes to hear it couple of times per day. It's his favorite story to read before bedtime. He said he likes it because he sees himself as the little star, his mom as the Moon Fairy and his dad as the Sun Prince. We discuss about story's message regularly, regardless of his favorite topic of the moment.

Shine: Why Don't Moon Fairy and Sun Prince Live Together?

Author: Polona Kisovec

Edited by Jolanda Vidic

Translated by Urška Charney

Proofread by Noah Charney

Illustrations by Mark Jordan

Design and layout: Mark Jordan

Director: Polona Kisovec

Shine: Why Don't Moon Fairy and Sun Prince Live Together?

Thank you!

Moon Fairy, Sun Prince and their little Star would like to thank you for reading their story and for letting them be a part of your life.

Their sincerest wish is that they were able to help you all find and ignite your unique light and express the love you feel for each-other. The love for your Star, that is here to stay forever.

They will be smiling upon you and your Star from behind the moonlight and sunshine.

»When something leaves a mark in your heart, it is there to stay forever.«

Moon Fairy was a playful and free-spirited girl. Night after night, she cast her silvery moonlight across the skies and onto the mountains and plains, the cities and villages. She spread her rays to light up the seas, lakes and rivers.

She loved counting the stars while swimming in the ocean, more than anything else. Her magical glow shone brightest then. One day, the words of her beauty resonated beyond the night's shadows, until they reached the light of day.

Sun Prince was one among many who heard about Moon Fairy's grace. So he wanted to meet her. One evening, as he bid farewell to the day on the western horizon, instead of laying down to rest, he set out straight into the night. He found the place where Moon Fairy loved to swim.

He was quietly in awe of how pretty and playful she was. Her magical glow enchanted him, and it wasn't long before he was in love.

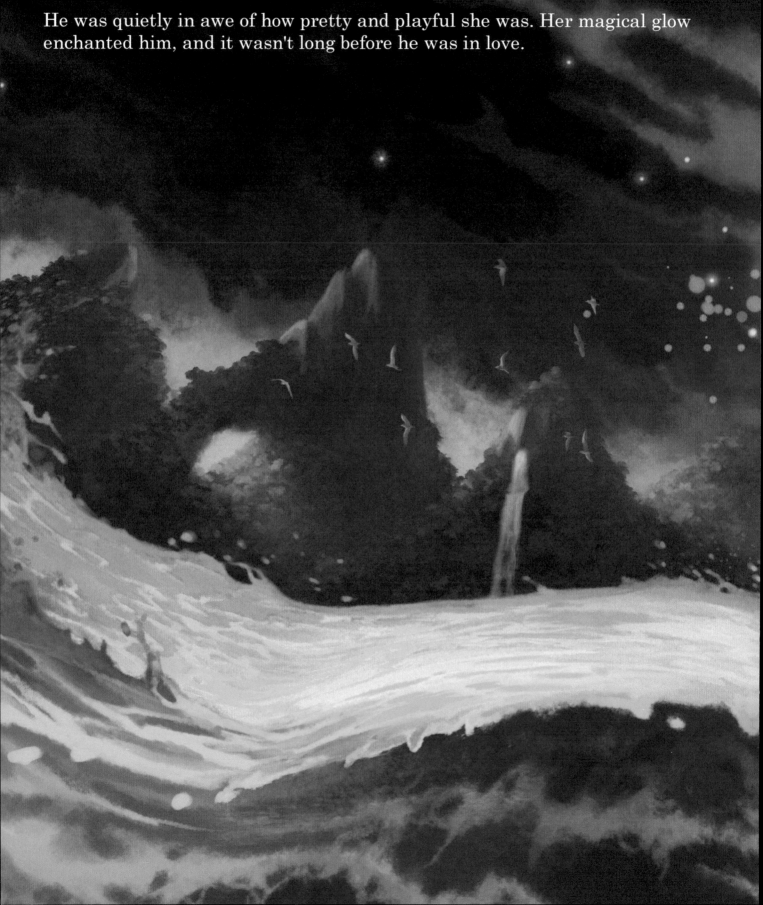

Sun Prince was eager to meet Moon Fairy, before she had to slip back into the sky at the break of day. But he was wise and clever, so he planned to meet her on the shore the following evening.

And so he did. That evening, like a thousand times before, Moon Fairy carefully took off her silvery gown and swam into the dark seas. Suddenly, Sun Prince emerged from his hideout, grabbed the clothes, hid behind the rock again and waited.

At the break of dawn, Moon Fairy reached the waterside, only to notice that her clothes were missing. She looked all over the shore, but they were nowhere to be found. »I can't return back to the sky without my clothes,« she thought to herself, while searching. And there he stood. Sun Prince, as bright as ever.

Moon Fairy was delighted to see her garments in his hands. They smiled to each other. Sun Prince told her that he had hidden her clothes only because he couldn't think of other ways to catch her before her departure.

They agreed to see each other again the next morning. Over many days, Sun Prince got up earlier than usual, to be able to chat and play with his lovely girlfriend. And each morning, Moon Fairy stayed longer, before flying back up into the skies. Their emotions grew stronger, and they fell ever more in love. They most enjoyed counting the shooting stars, while lying in the grass, with their arms around each other. They loved spending time together.

Day by day, their love flourished. Love between the golden and silvery light, between Sun Prince and Moon Fairy. Love between day and night.

One day, Sun Prince proposed that Moon Fairy should stay with him. He wanted them to live together and shine down on Earth, as one.

Moon Fairy was overjoyed by his words, for she loved Sun Prince. She also was hoping to spend more time with him. That day, Moon Fairy remained and did not leave for the skies. She stayed on Earth, and so did Sun Prince.

Their love gleamed not only in the morning, but provided warmth for nature during daytime, and painted the most breathtaking sunsets before night.

And at night, the silvery-golden light of their love filled up the skies. Moon Fairy continued to twinkle down from among the stars, and swim in the ocean, while Sun Prince enjoyed her company upon the shore. They couldn't have been happier together!

During these beautiful moments, when their light gleamed brightest, Moon Fairy's silvery glow interlaced with Sun Prince's golden rays. A miracle happened. From this wonderful light, a tiny little star was born. And it was named just like you.

Sun Prince and Moon Fairy loved their little star. Their joy was as infinite as the universe.

After a while, the days on Earth grew
hotter and hotter. Sun Prince and
Moon Fairy tried to glow as bright
as before. They tried to keep up with
their duties on Earth, and play with
their little star... But, the more they
tried, the hotter it was, and so they
grew tired and empty of the sparks
that once ignited their hearts.

They saw that their light was no longer bright.
That left them sad, and slowly their glow began
to weaken even further.

Nothing could cheer up Moon Fairy, not even swimming with her little star.Her face was ever paler, the nights ever darker. And Sun Prince, who once enjoyed watching his beloved Moon Fairy and little star, as they swam in the ocean each morning, grew ever sleepier. His sunny glow faded, and the days darkened.

One morning, when Moon Fairy was due to brighten up the sky with Sun Prince, her silvery light shut off altogether. She was no longer able to shine alongside Sun Prince in the daytime.

Seeing this, Sun Prince froze with fear that he may forever lose his beloved fairy. So he planned to cast his own light upon her in the evening, in hopes that she could spend time with him in the daytime.

In the evening, Moon Fairy headed to the skies without her magical silvery glow. Sun Prince summoned all that was left of his golden glow, to be able to shine upon her. They felt ever more lost.

At night, Moon Fairy could no longer swim in the ocean, carefree and nude. Her silvery glow, with which she had once illuminated her precious little star, was gone. It worried her, when she saw the prince wasting his last sun rays on her. The days of laughter were over. They no longer looked forward to the days and nights. »I must return into the night, and find my light again. Without it, I am just an invisible reflection of your rays,« Moon Fairy confessed sadly to Sun Prince.

Moon Fairy and Sun Prince realized that they could not go on like this, and could not live together anymore. »Sadly, we can't shine together anymore. But our love gave us the most precious gifts of all – our little star.«

Moon Fairy and Sun Prince aspired to be happy again. Moon Fairy wished to embellish the night's sky with her silvery glow, and swim freely through the peaceful seas again, while Sun Prince looked forward to waking the day with his golden rays of light.

They hugged their sweet little star and said: »There are millions of stars in the sky, but for us, you will always be the brightest of them all. The love of Sun Prince and Moon Fairy will always live in you. It will forever keep you warm, and your twinkling light will always bring joy to our hearts.« They hugged her so hard that one of her points forever left a mark in their hearts. And when something leaves a mark in your heart, it is there to stay forever.

Moon Fairy and Sun Prince now live separately, but they still greet each other every day, when the night falls and the day wakes. Meanwhile, their little star grows without a care, for in daylight she is kept warm by Sun Prince's golden rays, and at night she is gently caressed by Moon Fairy's silvery glow.

The little star twinkles brighter and brighter by the day, and with every smile she sprinkles stardust across the Earth, painting smiles on all the animals and people.

Made in the USA
Las Vegas, NV
20 November 2023

81258574R00024